The Synchronicity Experience

Practical Spirituality...Holistic Lifestyle

*Conscious Living
Contemporary
Meditation*

BALANCE * WHOLENESS * FULFILLMENT

Synchronicity Foundation International

Also by, about or based on the work of M.C. Cannon (Master Charles):

The Bliss of Freedom
A Contemporary Mystic's Enlightening Journey

Sourcing The Moment

The Synchronicity Guidebook

Synchronicity Foundation International
P.O. Box 694
Nellysford, VA 22958

The Library of Congress Control Number: 2002090545

ISBN Number 1-884068-81-2

This book is dedicated to
wholeness
and
unity consciousness.....
the fulfillment of being human.

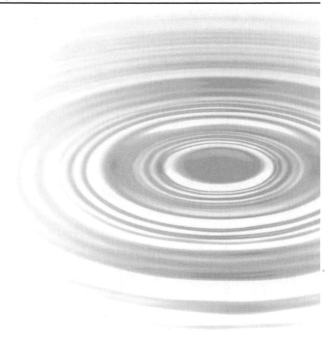

Table of Contents

Preface

Through balance..... wholeness.
In wholeness..... fulfillment.

It has been said that the eternal questions of human existence all have the same answer..... fulfillment. The search for fulfillment is the animating force underlying all life experience. Whether we are looking for love, power, prosperity or knowledge..... the journey is always about fulfillment. Yet, few understand that the fulfillment we seek outside ourselves, ultimately can only be found within, at the core of our human reality..... One Source Consciousness.

In the most ancient times and cultures upon this planet, The Great Wisdom Traditions of human experience have delineated awareness or Source consciousness as the foundation for human fulfillment. According to these traditions, awareness is actualized through a conscious lifestyle which includes meditation as its interior expression along with a comprehensive focus upon balance in every aspect of the exterior expression of daily life. In its traditional context, such a lifestyle was possible only within the confines of very structured, monastic communities which remained entirely separate and distinct from the culture at large. Obviously, it was a way of life reserved only for the few who were prepared to endure its rigors.

In our modern age, such contexts are virtually non-existent and yet the human aspiration for fulfillment is as universal and compelling as ever. As modern technology has evolved, the possibilities for human creative unfoldment have vastly expanded. On the other hand, that same technology has created enormous challenges in its wake when we consider human energetic reality. The world of today is not the same world, energetically speaking, as the world of thousands of years ago, when conscious living and meditative practices originated.

In today's world, we are individually and collectively surrounded by a vast energetic network or grid that crisscrosses the globe and powers the innumerable electronic devices, machines, information systems and infrastructure that literally supports life in these times. Radio, television and microwaves invisibly permeate the environment, and a human population exceeding seven billion with its attendant density and conflict create a global energetic reality unprecedented in its negative and stressful impact. Thus, for anyone endeavoring to create balance, wholeness and fulfillment, the ancient meditative paradigms fall short. They were simply not designed for the world we live in today. Those attempting to live consciously in today's world with ancient practices and technologies, more often than not, abort the journey in frustration.

Thus, the question of how to experience fulfillment and wholeness in the midst of an increasingly complex and fragmented world, has become one of the most challenging issues of our time. It was to address this challenge that M.C. Cannon (affectionately known as

Master Charles), created The Synchronicity Experience, including Synchronicity Conscious Living Integrative Lifestyle and Synchronicity Contemporary Meditation, nearly twenty years ago.

Based on The Synchronicity Holistic Cosmology of Reality, as outlined in the pages of this book, Synchronicity Conscious Living Integrative Lifestyle and Contemporary Meditation provides a comprehensive and practical means to deliver balance to every aspect of life. In addition, all Synchronicity Products and Services have as their foundation Synchronicity vibrational entrainment technology, a precision equilibration technology on audio CD's or cassettes which balances the brain hemispheres and delivers holistic awareness effortlessly and consistently. At the same time, this cutting edge technology harmonizes the chaotic environmental energies that impact us, allowing the meditator to experience the holistic awareness and bliss that is the hallmark of precision meditation. A Synchronicity Contemporary Meditation CD, along with instructions for its usage, is included with this book to provide the direct experience of holistic awareness.

Thus, The Synchronicity Experience is a comprehensive system that consciously addresses all aspects of holistic human experience and when incorporated into daily life, delivers fulfillment. Designed for the times in which we live, it both acknowledges the ancient model and yet includes the contemporary. As such, it is the experience whose time has come and that is its brilliance.

In the recognition of our Oneness, we are pleased to present The Synchronicity Experience, Contemporary Meditation and Conscious Living. While it serves as an introduction to The Synchronicity Paradigm, it nevertheless includes the most comprehensive and contemporary approach to human fulfillment available today. As Master Charles has said, the primary intention in human experience is to fully recognize our Oneness. It is in this spirit that you are welcomed to the world of Synchronicity.

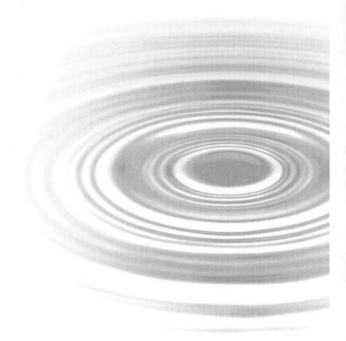

Introduction

Stop..... look..... listen. Here and now.....
in this moment..... there is only One.

The Synchronicity Experience, which includes Synchronicity Contemporary Meditation and Synchronicity Conscious Living Integrative Lifestyle, was originated by M.C. Cannon (affectionately known as Master Charles), an American mystic and master of meditation.

Following a formal education in the arts with an emphasis on Comparative Religion and Philosophy, Master Charles furthered his education over many years in India as a disciple of the renowned Eastern mystic, Paramahansa Muktananda and was ordained as a Vedic monk.

After Muktananda's death, he relinquished the eastern orthodox monastic lifestyle and returned to the United States where he endeavored to create a synthesis between the ancient mystical / philosophical traditions of the East and the science and technology of the West. He established Synchronicity Foundation as a religious, educational, non-profit organization in 1983. The Synchronicity Paradigm was first published and presented in 1984.

It is the basis of the Synchronicity Experience. It includes: The Holistic Cosmology of Reality, Synchronicity Contemporary Meditation and Synchronicity Conscious Living Integrative Lifestyle. It is a comprehensive system for the actualization of holistic human experience and its resultant fulfillment. In this context, the classical journey of spiritual enlightenment has been given a contemporary and technological update, enabling new generations and cultures to experience this timeless wisdom. Master Charles' seeming abandonment of traditional religious contexts in favor of the contemporary approach, makes him one of the most innovative spiritual teachers of our times.

The Synchronicity Experience has been a great success for one simple reason - it works. It is precise and efficient, taking far less time and effort than classical systems of meditation and conscious living. This acceleration factor is one of the principle differences between The Synchronicity Experience and classical, orthodox, non-technological methods. The speed with which measurable changes occur in one's awareness has been validated by measurement of the brain-wave patterns produced by regular participants in The Synchronicity Experience. These were compared to the measurements produced by those using classical methods. Our findings empirically validate the assertion first advanced by Master Charles in The Synchronicity Paradigm, that The Synchronicity Experience yields a four-fold acceleration factor over classical methods of meditation and conscious living.

This book has been designed for the general reader and does not require either a background in Eastern philosophy or Western science. Yet, those who have experience in these areas will find the work of Master Charles and Synchronicity Foundation brings unprecedented clarity to the often "mystifying" subjects of holistic awareness, meditation and conscious living. Where appropriate, correspondences between classical and contemporary methods have been made, in order to assist the reader in understanding how the two systems complement and validate each other.

For almost twenty years, Master Charles and Synchronicity Foundation have continued to research and develop contemporary techniques for the expansion and integration of holistic awareness. New explorations in the use of vibrational entrainment technology along with the application of cutting edge integrative protocols have created a uniquely transformational experience for those interested in wholeness and the fulfillment of being human. Our observations of the transformational journeys of hundreds of people over the years have continued to validate the contemporary approach of The Synchronicity Experience put forth in our original publications.

Included with this book is a Synchronicity Contemporary Meditation soundtrack on CD. Our intention is to share with you the tangible experience of the transformational system that is delineated in this book. Detailed instructions for its usage are also included.

This book is divided into seven sections as follows:

Living with balance in an imbalanced world is one of the major challenges we face in these modern times. While meditation, along with a conscious living integrative lifestyle, is considered the primary context for balance in human experience, it has remained largely the province of Eastern or esoteric spiritual and philosophic traditions. This has made conscious living far less practical and accessible to many who would otherwise benefit greatly from its regular experience.

The advent of The Synchronicity Paradigm, has for the first time, updated this time-tested and experientially validated approach into a modern, scientific context, thus making it available to anyone endeavoring to experience holistic awareness and human fulfillment. Both in the pages of this book, as well as the included CD, you will have an opportunity to understand and experientially validate The Synchronicity Paradigm for yourself. It is in this spirit that we present this introduction to The Synchronicity Experience - Conscious Living and Contemporary Meditation.

Part One

*Synchronicity Foundation
and
Synchronicity Sanctuary*

Here and now..... in this moment.....
I am Source..... all is Source.....
this truth is self-evident.

Synchronicity Foundation

Synchronicity Foundation was created in 1983 by M.C. Cannon (Master Charles) and associates as a not-for-profit, tax exempt 501(c)(3), religious, educational organization. Its founding intention, as stated in its Articles of Incorporation, is Conscious Living through Contemporary Meditation. Its creation is based upon The Synchronicity Paradigm, originated by M.C. Cannon and includes the following:

1. The Holistic Cosmology of Reality - a multi-dimensional model with one consciousness as the Source.

2. Conscious Living Integrative Lifestyle and Contemporary Meditation as the means of actualizing The Holistic Cosmology of Reality in human experience.

The founders endeavored to create a contemporary, Western lifestyle for actualizing holistic experience in an acknowledgment of the failure of idealistic religion and philosophic models to do so. They also acknowledged the schism between religious and scientific experience and endeavored to unify them. They intended to create a daily lifestyle that would actualize and validate The Holistic Cosmology of Reality with one consciousness as the Source, as advanced by scholars and informed academia and encapsulated in The Synchronicity Paradigm. M.C. Cannon was chosen to fulfill the role of mentor as delineated in The Synchronicity Paradigm in recognition of:

1. His acknowledged state of actualized wholeness..... he had validated the model in his own experience.

2. His life experience, which included a background in Comparative Religion and Philosophy with specialization in holistic models of reality with one consciousness as the Source.

Synchronicity Sanctuary

Synchronicity Sanctuary, located in The Blue Ridge Mountains of central Virginia, was created as the headquarters for Synchronicity Foundation. This four hundred fifty acre, rural, sylvan retreat has been developed over the years to include residential facilities for the monastic community and guest facilities for retreat participants.

Herein, The Synchronicity Community actualizes Synchronicity Conscious Living Integrative Lifestyle on a daily basis through a full daily schedule which addresses both interior and exterior balance. Anchored in the practice of Synchronicity Contemporary Meditation, community members staff the Foundation and collectively share their experience with Foundation members and the general public. The individualized, interior focus provided by the daily practice of Synchronicity Contemporary Meditation, together with the exterior focus in relation to the world at large, fulfills the founders' intention of a Conscious Living Integrative Lifestyle that actualizes The Holistic Model of Reality.

In almost twenty years, The Synchronicity Community, under the continuing guidance of M.C. Cannon (Master Charles), has validated, refined and evolved The Synchronicity Experience. The result has been no less than holistic fulfillment.

Part Two

The Synchronicity Paradigm

I am Source. I am eternally creative.
I manifest all and everything..... as myself.
I am the One and Only.

The Synchronicity Paradigm

The Synchronicity Paradigm acknowledges the three principles of valid science:

1. Paradigm / Model
2. Apprehension / Experimental Data Collection
3. Confirmation / Falsification / Individual and Collective

According to contemporary standards of empirical investigation, there are three principles or criteria that must be present in any valid model of scientific inquiry. First, there must be the formulation and delineation of the paradigm / model that one proposes to validate. Secondly, the paradigm / model must be supported by the apprehension and collection of experiential data. Thirdly, the methodology and results must be made available to others for confirmation or falsification. These three principles form the basis of scientific inquiry and validation for any paradigm / model. The Synchronicity Paradigm conforms to these three principles and through them has demonstrated its validity.

The Synchronicity Paradigm
Delineation

The Synchronicity Paradigm has three main components or sections as follows:

1. The Synchronicity Holistic Cosmology of Reality
2. Synchronicity Contemporary Meditation
3. Synchronicity Conscious Living Integrative Lifestyle

Herewith follows a detailed delineation of each component or section.

The Synchronicity Holistic Cosmology of Reality
Fulfillment Through Wholeness
There Is Only One

One Consciousness

The Synchronicity Holistic Cosmology of Reality is based on a distillation of The Great Wisdom Traditions in combination with modern science. This model is likewise acknowledged by modern scholars and informed academia. The model is termed "holistic" because it establishes one consciousness as the Source, substratum or Ground of Being. Further, it is a multi-dimensional consciousness that encompasses all experience from dense to subtle..... from dense, physical matter to subtle energetic experience..... from the macrocosm to the microcosm..... from the universal to the individual.

The Synchronicity Holistic Cosmology of Reality delineates seven dimensions of the multi-dimensional whole from subtle to dense. They are: The Void, The Supracausal, The Causal, The Subtle, The Mental, The Emotional, and The Physical.

The Void

The word Void, is used to symbolize the Ultimate Reality beyond all experience. It is the womb of all experience, thus it is termed The Pregnant Void, because all possibility is inherent within it. The One is only ever The One. Eternal delight is its inherent, holistic fulfillment.

The primary intention in consciousness is to fully be itself. Out of The Void, the One eternally delighting consciousness actualizes The Creation Game..... The Play of Consciousness..... governed by The Relative Field as the arena of all experience..... the arena of itself as one consciousness through which it continually experiences and magnifies its delight. In order to be itself, it must become itself..... all experience is therefore relative..... being is only in relation to becoming.

The Relative Field

One Source Consciousness creates The Relative Field as the arena of all experience. All experience is relative. This is polarized, multi-dimensional reality from subtle to dense. Yet, there is truly only

One Consciousness as both relative polarities. Unity and Diversity..... Being and Becoming..... Subject and Object..... Positive and Negative..... Interior and Exterior..... are the same One Source Consciousness. Within the most subtle dimensions of reality, where there is more relative balance, consciousness is aware of itself, or in the recognition of itself as one consciousness. This is termed wholeness or unity consciousness. Within the densest dimensions of reality, where there is more relative imbalance, consciousness forfeits awareness and is not fully in the recognition of itself. This is termed fragmentation or disunity. Yet, in truth, there is only One Consciousness and disunity is illusion or pretense. Further, all experience is a process of progressive integrative wholeness through all the dimensions and illusion yields to truth as Source consciousness recognizes itself as One. Ultimately, wholeness equals fulfillment.

The Relative Field governs all experience. Within The Relative Field, the negative polarity dominates the positive polarity. Becoming dominates being, diversity dominates unity, the manifest dominates the unmanifest in order to create form over formlessness and universal manifestation. Yet, this is the dominance of illusion over truth. But, even in pretense, The One remains The One. The negative polarity is the dominant default polarity and the positive polarity is the non-dominant opposite. Thus, One Consciousness as the Source creates and experiences itself through The Relative Field. Within the subtlest dimensions, there is less polarized dominance and therefore more balance and holistic awareness. Within the densest dimensions, there is more polarized dominance and therefore more imbalance and less holistic awareness. Herein, One Consciousness, through illusion, obscures itself from itself in order that it might truthfully recognize itself and magnify its inherent delight in the process. Thus, The Creation Game is a process of ever-increasing integrative wholeness and fulfillment.

All human experience conforms to this holistic model and its principles from The Void through The Relative Field. Human experience is thus also a process of progressive integrative wholeness from dense to subtle and balance is ever-increasing over imbalance as a constant. The result of wholeness is fulfillment or the constancy of delight which is intrinsic to One Consciousness. Yet, human experience is multi-dimensional and multi-leveled which validates the diversity of unity.

The actualization of a progressive integrative wholeness is the play of consciousness in human experience. It is The Creation Game for the fun of it. Since delight is intrinsic to One Consciousness, how could it be otherwise? Wholeness is proportional to balance in The Relative Field and therefore the lifestyle model of an integrative wholeness must be based on balance. Since the negative polarity is dominant, in order to actualize balance, emphasis must be placed on the non-dominant opposite..... or the positive polarity. The emphasis thus is Being over Becoming..... positive over negative..... subject over object..... interior over exterior. In this way, both polarities are equalized and balance is actualized. The resultant experience is progressive integrative wholeness and unity consciousness. The lifestyle model calls for a subjective science to daily address the interior and an objective science to daily address the exterior. Balanced emphasis thus evolves a progressive integrative wholeness rather than an imbalanced, polarized isolationism that is either interior or exterior in its focus. Again, fulfillment in human experience is through wholeness.

Contemporary Meditation
Interior Science

Synchronicity Contemporary Meditation, created by Master Charles, is the interior science of The Synchronicity Paradigm Lifestyle Model, to be utilized on a daily basis. This form of meditation utilizes vibrational entrainment technology to bring precision to the meditative experience. Through subtle vibrational entrainment, the relative polarities are balanced. Since meditation is basically a balancing technique, this form of meditation is merely contemporary meditation that includes scientific technology. It is best understood with the human brain as an example. The Relative Field is represented within the human bi-cameral brain. The right hemisphere is the subjective or positive polarity and the left hemisphere is the objective or negative polarity. Since the negative polarity is dominant, human experience is left-brain dominant. Meditation, with its subjective focus, emphasizes the non-dominant opposite and thus balances the two hemispheres of the brain. This is termed "whole-brain synchrony" and the resultant human experience of this balance is wholeness or unity consciousness. Within a daily lifestyle application, Synchronicity Contemporary Meditation delivers precision to the progressive process of integrative wholeness.

The use of vibrational entrainment technology in Synchronicity Contemporary Meditation brings precision to the balancing process of meditation. This can be validated with scientific observation of the human brain. An EEG machine or computerized brain monitor is utilized for such validation. As brain-wave patterns (Beta, Alpha, Theta, Delta) decelerate, whole-brain synchrony or hemispheric balance proportionally increases.

This is wholeness through balance. The resultant experience is multi-dimensional awareness as separation (imbalance) decreases and unity (balance) increases. This is the actualization of an integrative wholeness based on balance within The Relative Field. Synchronicity vibrational entrainment technology brings precision to this balancing meditative process. A four-fold acceleration factor has been validated over non-technological forms of meditation.

Thus, the interior focus of The Synchronicity Paradigm Lifestyle Model is actualized through the daily use of Synchronicity Contemporary Meditation. Again..... wholeness through balance delivers human fulfillment.

Conscious Living Integrative Lifestyle
Exterior Science

Synchronicity Conscious Living Integrative Lifestyle, created by Master Charles, is the exterior science of The Synchronicity Paradigm Lifestyle Model, to be actualized on a daily basis. It delivers the exterior balance necessary to an integrative wholeness. In combination, Synchronicity Contemporary Meditation and Synchronicity Conscious Living Integrative Lifestyle, deliver both the interior and exterior balance that is necessary to a progressive experience of integrative, multi-dimensional wholeness and human fulfillment.

Synchronicity Conscious Living Integrative Lifestyle is living with awareness. Thus, it is termed conscious living. Awareness however, is proportional to balance in The Relative Field. Just as meditation actualizes balance through an interior focus, conscious living actualizes balance through an exterior focus.

The negative polarity is dominant in The Relative Field. This is unconscious experience. To actualize balance, emphasis must be on the non-dominant opposite or the positive polarity. This is conscious experience. Thus, the term Conscious Living. In Synchronicity Conscious Living Integrative Lifestyle, the emphasis is therefore directed to the positive polarity. Then, through balance, the progressive process of integrative wholeness is actualized with resultant human fulfillment.

Synchronicity Conscious Living Integrative Lifestyle can best be understood through a dimensional representation. It begins with the denser dimensions of human multi-dimensionality..... The Physical, The Emotional and The Mental. These are termed The Primary Trinity in The Synchronicity Holistic Cosmology of Reality, because they are the foundation of our human multi-dimensionality. Until The Primary Trinity is balanced, it is impossible to actualize balance within the subtler dimensions..... subtle, causal and supracausal. Therefore, wholeness or multi-dimensional actualization begins with an emphasis on The Primary Trinity of the physical, emotional and mental dimensions of human experience.

In each of these three dimensions, the negative polarity is dominant and emphasis must be placed on the non-dominant opposite or positive polarity in order to actualize balance and integrative wholeness. When The Primary Trinity is maintained in balance, there is Harmonic Coherence and the subtler dimensions then actualize as a result. Again, this is the process of ever increasing integrative wholeness. Thus, the importance of balancing The Primary Trinity. Positive or conscious emphasis is always the key to balance.

The Physical Dimension

The Relative Field of positive and negative polarity is represented in the Physical Dimension through the biochemistry of the physical body. This can be simply expressed as alkaline to acid or insulin to glucose. Negative polarity dominance results in an imbalance of acid over alkaline or glucose over insulin. Emphasizing the non-dominant opposite of alkaline or insulin thus delivers physical dimensional balance. This is consciously actualized through nutrition and exercise. Thus, the necessity of a balanced diet - alkaline to acid, insulin to glucose and balanced exercise - activity to inertia, within a twenty-four hour time-frame.

Synchronicity Conscious Living Integrative Lifestyle requires vigilance to insure that a balanced biochemistry is maintained in The Physical Dimension through balanced nutrition and exercise. The Zone Diet System, created by Dr. Barry Sears, is recommended for its scientific precision in maintaining physical dimensional balance through nutrition and exercise in Synchronicity Conscious Living Integrative Lifestyle.

The Emotional Dimension

The Relative Field of positive and negative polarity is represented in The Emotional Dimension through the hormonal system. Within the progressive process of integrative wholeness, hormonal balance is actualized through biochemical balance or physical dimensional balance interacts with and actualizes emotional dimensional balance. In addition, vigilance must be brought to emotional expression. Negative polarity dominance results in an imbalance of negative over positive emotional expression. This is fear-based emotion over love-based emotion. Emphasizing the non-dominant opposite of love-based emotion over fear-based emotion delivers Emotional Dimensional balance. This is consciously actualized through consistent positive emotional expression. Emphasis is consciously placed on positive emotional flow as in contentment, compassion and love within a twenty-four hour time frame. The result is Emotional Dimensional balance.

Synchronicity Conscious Living Integrative Lifestyle requires vigilance to insure that a balanced hormonal system and balanced emotional expression is maintained within The Emotional Dimension. The result is ever-increasing integrative wholeness.

The Mental Dimension

The Relative Field of positive and negative polarity is represented in The Mental Dimension in the neurochemical system. Within the progressive process of integrative wholeness, biochemical Physical Dimensional balance interacts with and actualizes hormonal Emotional Dimensional balance, which in turn, interacts with and actualizes neurochemical Mental Dimensional balance. In addition, vigilance must be brought to mental expression. Negative polarity dominance results in an imbalance of negative over positive mental expression. This is negative data and thought construct over positive data and thought construct. Emphasizing the non-dominant opposite of positive, affirmative data and thought construct over negative data and thought construct delivers Mental Dimensional balance. This is consciously actualized through consistent positive, life-affirmative mental expression. Simply put, this is the necessity of positive thinking. This is actualized through the affirmation process. Emphasis is consciously directed to life-affirmative data and thought processes within a twenty-four time-frame. The result is Mental Dimensional balance.

Synchronicity Conscious Living Integrative Lifestyle requires vigilance to insure that a balanced neurochemical system and balanced mental expression is maintained within The Mental Dimension. The result is ever-increasing integrative wholeness.

The Subtle Dimensions
Subtle, Causal and Supracausal

The Relative Field governs all dimensions of the multi-dimensional whole. The subtle dimensions are termed subtle, because relative polarities therein are subtly represented. Within the progressive process of integrative wholeness, the subtle dimensions transcend and include the dense dimensions. Thus, the physical, emotional and mental cognition of the dense dimensions is transcended and subtle energetic information replaces dense data and thought construct. The Relative Field of positive and negative polarity is represented in the subtle dimensions as subtle energetic information. This is experienced as vibrational oscillation between the relative polarities. The relative oscillation or the frequency of vibration of The Relative Field proportionally accelerates from dense to subtle dimensions. The subtle dimensions therefore vibrate at the speed of light and beyond, toward infinite velocity. The resultant balance of this accelerated frequency of vibration delivers proportional, holistic awareness expansion. Herein, the space-time continuum is bent and reality becomes more non-linear or simultaneous in experience. The past, present and future of linear time-space merge into the eternal now of simultaneous reality. This is experienced as the constancy or continuity of unity consciousness or wholeness. One Consciousness is thus less obscured from itself in the subtler dimensions and more in the recognition of itself as One. Again, ultimately there is only One.

The Subtle Dimension is marked by a detachment from the denser dimensions of The Primary Trinity - physical, emotional and mental. This detached observation or more holistic perspective is termed witness consciousness. In subtle dimensional actualization, one is a detached witness of the physical, emotional and mental dimensions. This is the experience of more holistic awareness or Source Consciousness. The subtle dimensions are actualized by consistency of balance in The Primary Trinity of the physical, emotional and mental dimensions. Through consistency or duration in balance, there is Harmonic Coherence and the momentum of Harmonic Coherence as a vibrational frequency actualizes the subtler dimensions.

Likewise, consistency or duration within the Subtle Dimension actualizes the Causal Dimension, which in turn, actualizes the Supracausal Dimension.

The Causal Dimension is represented as an expansion of witness consciousness into unity consciousness as the progressive process of ever-increasing integrative wholeness continues to unfold. In the Causal Dimension, the negative polarity still slightly dominates the positive polarity - or becoming (form) slightly dominates being (formlessness). This is also an experience of holistic absorption with form. The frequency of vibration in The Relative Field is beyond the speed of light and there is thus the experience of simultaneous reality..... subject and object are not separated but simultaneous in experience.

The Supracausal Dimension is represented as a further expansion of unity consciousness as the progressive process of ever-increasing integrative wholeness continues to unfold. In the Supracausal Dimension, the positive polarity slightly dominates the negative polarity - or being (formlessness) slightly dominates becoming (form). This is the experience of holistic absorption without form. The frequency of vibration in The Relative Field is approaching infinite velocity and there is thus the experience of simultaneous reality - subject and object are a unified whole. This is the experience of One Consciousness fully in the recognition of itself. This is the culmination of the progressive process of integrative wholeness or the constancy of unity consciousness. Again, ultimately, there is only One, as consciousness fulfills its intention to fully be itself. This is ultimate human fulfillment.

The Creation Game - A Play of Consciousness
Truth and Illusion
Bliss Magnification

There is only One..... The One is only ever The One. Eternal delight or the bliss of Oneness, is its inherent holistic fulfillment. Its primary intention is to fully be itself and in order to be itself, it must become itself. All experience is thus relative and The Relative Field is created as the arena of experience.

Through all the dimensions of the multi-dimensional whole, The Relative Field represents the experience of Being in relation to Becoming. It is the eternal oscillation of polarized wholeness. This is The Creation Game as The Play of Consciousness - or the play of truth and illusion..... being and becoming.

There is only One, yet in order to experience itself, it must pretend not to be itself. This is illusion or becoming. It is the negative polarity. Yet, in the eternal oscillation, being oscillates with becoming, truth oscillates with illusion..... the positive oscillates with the negative. When being dominates becoming, when truth dominates illusion, there is recognition - The One recognizes itself..... unity experiences itself as diversity. The resultant awareness expansion is bliss magnification. Thus, The Creation Game, The Play of Consciousness, is an eternal process of bliss magnification. Since delight (bliss) is inherent in consciousness - the creation cannot be different from The Creator. Recognition is thus always bliss magnification. This is the nature of relative experience.

The oscillation of relative polarities is operative throughout the multi-dimensional whole. It is The Play of Consciousness in each dimension. Consciousness is creative, ever presenting new forms of itself..... illusions..... that it might recognize itself ever anew..... truth..... and consistently magnify its bliss. Within the progressive process of integrative wholeness, truth and illusion progressively balance each other or become simultaneous in reality. This is the experience of wholeness or unity consciousness.

In the denser dimensions, illusion is more dominant through imbalance and bliss magnification is thus minimal. In the subtler dimensions, truth and illusion become more simultaneous through balance and bliss magnification is thus maximum. This is the progressive process of ever-increasing human fulfillment. When one is consistently multi-dimensionally whole, there is the constancy of unity consciousness and blissful fulfillment.

Wholeness is blissful fulfillment. Again, ultimately there is only One, and to live with holistic awareness is blissful.

The Synchronicity Paradigm's Holistic Lifestyle, daily actualized through Synchronicity Contemporary Meditation and Synchronicity Conscious Living Integrative Lifestyle, progressively delivers the experience of wholeness and blissful fulfillment. It actualizes the fullness of human experience as One Consciousness in the recognition of itself.

The Pathology of Fragmentation
Wholeness Through Balance
Fragmentation Through Imbalance

The Synchronicity Holistic Model of Reality delineates the actualization of wholeness through balance within The Relative Field that governs all experience. It also delineates the actualization of fragmentation through imbalance in The Relative Field.

The One Source Consciousness must first Become what it is not in order to Be what it is. Being is always in relation to Becoming. This is relative experience through which the primary intention in consciousness is fulfilled. Relative experience is a progressive process of ever-increasing integrative wholeness through which consciousness builds a momentum. In the initial stages, negative polarity dominance is to the extreme. Becoming dominates Being - illusion dominates truth - and this is represented as imbalance within The Relative Field. As relative experience progresses, a momentum toward positive polarity dominance increases - Being equalizes Becoming - truth equalizes illusion. Thus, in more evolved stages, there is balance and wholeness. Yet, the initial unevolved stages remain imbalanced and the experience of consciousness is fragmented therein. This experience is termed The Pathology of Fragmentation.

As in any disease there are specific symptoms, The Pathology of Fragmentation also has specific symptoms - the symptoms of fragmented, imbalanced experience. They are generally delineated as follows:

1) Polarized Isolationism
2) Duality, Separation and Egocentricity
3) Obsessive Narcissism and Selfishness

Polarized Isolationism

When one polarity dominates the other within The Relative Field, there is polarized imbalance. If this polarized imbalance continues in duration, it becomes polarized isolationism. Since the negative polarity is dominant by virtue of manifestation, polarized isolationism is predominantly to the negative. The negative polarity is Becoming..... the external..... the objective..... the illusion. It is what consciousness is not in relation to what it is. Since holistic awareness is forfeited in imbalance, polarized isolationism is fragmented experience. In human experience, the fragmentation of polarized isolationism progresses to illusory separation and duality. Thus, it actualizes the next symptom within The Pathology of Fragmentation..... Egocentricity.

Egocentricity, Separation and Duality

Sustained polarized isolationism to the negative delivers a progressive identification with illusion. Illusory duality dominates and there is separation. The illusion of the ego and egocentric experience emerges. The ego is a false and illusory identity as other than One Source Consciousness. Herein is a seeming separation of polarity within The Relative Field..... Being is now separated and different from Becoming..... subject and object are now separated and different from each other..... this is separate from that..... the I is separate from the It. In human experience, this is illusory duality. I (as subject) am separate from It..... all and everything (as object)..... or I (subject..... positive..... being), am separate and different from what I am not (object..... negative..... becoming). Herein is the human fragmentation of the exterior over the interior. Holistic awareness is forfeited and illusory duality dominates. This then, actualizes the next symptom of The Pathology of Fragmentation..... Obsessive Narcissism and Selfishness.

Obsessive Narcissism and Selfishness

Sustained egocentricity, duality and separation progress into an extremely isolated and polarized identification with dualistic illusion. Herein, the ego illusion is dominant. Holistic awareness is further forfeited and fragmentation reigns supreme. All experience is thus egocentric or self-centered as the illusory identity of the ego becomes obsessive. The ego is placed first and all else second. The result is obsessive focus on self or what is termed obsessive narcissism. This is selfish experience. It is fragmented and limited. It is extreme dualistic illusion.

The Remedy..... Awareness

There is a remedy to cure the disease of The Pathology of Fragmentation. It heals and eliminates all the symptoms..... polarized isolationism..... egocentricity..... duality..... separation..... obsessive narcissism and selfishness. The remedy is holistic awareness. It is actualized through balance in The Relative Field. First, balance must be actualized through emphasis on the non-dominant polarity..... the positive..... Being. A positive polarity focus must be brought to each dimension of The Primary Trinity..... physical, emotional and mental. As holistic awareness expands through relative balance, the subtle dimensions will likewise progressively actualize. Ultimately, there will be multi-dimensional actualization as fragmentation yields to wholeness. The result is human fulfillment with correspondent bliss magnification.

The Pathology of Fragmentation is a non-fulfilling human experience because holistic recognition and resultant bliss magnification are forfeited therein. If living with holistic awareness is blissful, then living without it is misery. Wholeness is thus satisfaction and fragmentation is dissatisfaction. One is pleasure, the other is pain. Again, the ecstasy or the agony of human experience.

Through balance in The Relative Field, holistic awareness is actualized. There is the recognition of One Consciousness. Illusion is relinquished. Truth remains..... there is only One..... and inherent delight is magnified as bliss. Thus, awareness is the remedy, the cure for The Pathology of Fragmentation.

The Role of the Mentor

Human experience is a progressive process of ever-increasing integrative wholeness through all the dimensions of the multi-dimensional whole. This progressive actualization proceeds from dense to subtle and everyone begins at level one..... The Primary Trinity..... or the denser dimensions of the Physical, Emotional and Mental. Because One Source Consciousness is the most obscured from itself in The Primary Trinity, The Pathology of Fragmentation is likewise the most pronounced or dominant therein. Thus, the mechanics of balance and progressive awareness expansion are the most challenging within these dimensions of human experience. Since One Source Consciousness is herein challenged with its illusions and holistic recognition and awareness are minimal, the role of the Mentor emerges as an evolutionary necessity. All of The Great Wisdom Traditions acknowledge the role of the Mentor and so also does The Synchronicity Paradigm.

Holistic Entrainment

In delineating the role of the Mentor, an analogy is often used. It is said that if one wants to get a suntan, one must place onself in the proximity of the sun. This analogy encapsulates the principle of holistic entrainment. First and foremost, the Mentor must be an holistic entrainment. What does this mean? The whole is greater than the sum of its parts. The experience of multi-dimensional wholeness then, has more power than fragmented and limited dimensional experience. This is represented in The Relative Field that governs all experience as the oscillation of polarity and its energetic frequency of vibration. The energetic frequency of vibration of multi-dimensional wholeness is beyond the speed of light toward infinite velocity. Thus, it has great power and vibrationally entrains all parts to it. This is the holistic momentum in Source Consciousness, or its primary intention to fully be itself. Again, it is a progressive process of ever-increasing integrative wholeness. Thus, constancy of multi-dimensional wholeness as an experience has great power as a vibrational frequency and serves as an entrainment..... holistic entrainment.

The Mentor, therefore, must first and foremost actualize a consistency of multi-dimensional wholeness which is expressed as holistic vibrational energetic entrainment. The Mentor must be an holistic vibrational energetic entrainment, which is based on the actualization of multi-dimensional integrative wholeness. The holistic energetic vibrational frequency of the Mentor then entrains all that it encounters to the same holistic energetic vibrational frequency. The Mentor energetically entrains balance and holistic awareness expansion in relative experience. Or..... the sun delivers the suntan.

It has also been said that "an I cannot see itself". In fragmented, egocentric experience, illusion dominates truth..... Source Consciousness therefore, is challenged in recognizing itself. Immersed in illusory duality, it cannot easily recognize its Oneness. Therefore, in its multi-dimensionality and progressive process of integrative wholeness, the more evolved forms of itself serve as holistic entrainments to the less evolved forms of itself. This is a further validation of its unity in diversity..... the one in the many. The Mentor then embodies evolved holistic experience and expresses it as holistic entrainment. Further, having actualized a consistent holistic experience through the progressive process of ever-increasing integrative wholeness, the Mentor can also be a Conscious Living Integrative Lifestyle and Meditation facilitator.

The role of the Mentor is similar in all aspects of human experience. If one wants to become a cook, a master cook mentor is necessary. One would not choose a plumber mentor if they wanted to become a cook. Likewise, if one wants to become whole, an holistic mentor is necessary. The result of such association will obviously be wholeness.

Thus, the role of the Mentor is clearly defined in The Synchronicity Paradigm.....

1) Consistent Holistic Experience
2) Holistic Vibrational Energetic Entrainment
3) Meditation and Conscious Living Integrative Lifestyle Mastery

When these criteria are fully actualized, the necessary role of the Mentor is fulfilled and serves its function within The Play of Consciousness. The result of such association then, must be progressive integrative wholeness and human fulfillment.

Fulfillment
Wholeness Equals Fulfillment

There is only One. One Source Consciousness eternally delights in Itself. Delight or fulfillment is intrinsic to wholeness. In truth, delight or fulfillment cannot be separated from consciousness. It is its nature to be fulfilled within itself. The creation is not different from the creator.

The Play of Consciousness, thus, is based in delight. It emerges from the inherent delight of One Source Consciousness and sustains its delight through all experience..... which is only the experience of itself. Thus, it continually magnifies its delight through all its experience. The Play of Consciousness is so termed because "play" is synonymous with delight. It is joyous experience. The Play of Consciousness is thus for the delight..... the joy..... the bliss of the experience. Since it cannot truthfully change what it is, it continually experiences more of itself. The Play of Consciousness continually magnifies its delight..... its joy..... its bliss. This is the fulfillment of its wholeness..... its Oneness.

The Play of Consciousness in human experience is the same. Fulfillment is through wholeness. Fulfillment is proportional to wholeness. Life is an experience to be truthfully lived for the joy of it..... for the bliss of it. Life truthfully lived..... life holistically lived, is a satisfying and pleasurable experience. It is delightfully, joyfully, blissfully fulfilling.

Yet, The Play of Consciousness is governed by The Relative Field and all experience is relative. In truth, there is only One Source Consciousness as both polarities. In illusion, there is other than One Source Consciousness in both polarities. In truthful experience, there is only One. Being and becoming..... subject and object..... positive and negative..... unity and diversity..... are the same One Source Consciousness. One Source Consciousness, thus in the recognition of itself, consistently magnifies its inherent delight. This is the holistically fulfilling experience of life for the joy of it..... for the bliss of it. Again, fulfillment is proportional to wholeness.

Through illusion, there is fragmentation. Yet, it is pretense. Being and Becoming..... subject and object..... positive and negative..... unity and diversity..... are seemingly separated and different from each other. Such illusory fragmentation is created through relative imbalance and wholeness is compromised. Herein, the negative..... objective..... diversity polarity dominates and Source Consciousness is obscured from itself. Delight..... joy..... bliss..... are proportionally forfeited in the process. This is fragmented experience, yet it is illusory. In truth, there is only One.

Thus, through illusion..... pretense..... One Source Consciousness plays a game of hide and seek with itself. It tricks itself, pretending to become other than it is..... in order that it might recognize itself..... experience itself..... as it is..... and in the process of the game..... magnify its bliss. Again, in truth, The Play of Consciousness is a game for the fun of it..... for the joy of it..... for the bliss of it. It is only an experience of bliss magnification.

Human experience..... all experience..... within The Play of Consciousness is a progressive process of ever-increasing integrative wholeness. Thus, it delivers ever-increasing fulfillment in terms of the constancy of delight, joy and bliss. Ultimately, in the actualization of consistent wholeness, there is fulfillment and life is a satisfying, pleasurable, joyous, delightful and blissful experience.

The Synchronicity Paradigm delineates fulfillment through wholeness. The actualization of wholeness through balance is the point of all experience..... including human experience. Thus, Synchronicity Conscious Living Integrative Lifestyle, combined with Synchronicity Contemporary Meditation daily lived, delivers the experience of holistic reality as The Play of One Consciousness..... or balance delivers wholeness and wholeness equals fulfillment. Again, The Synchronicity Paradigm delineates and validates fulfillment through wholeness. Life truthfully lived..... holistically lived..... is a blissfully fulfilling experience.

Part Three

Actualizing The Synchronicity Paradigm

The creation is not different from the creator.
Source creates Source..... the One in the many.
I am..... all is.

The Five Principles of Conscious Living

Five principles of conscious living have been delineated by Master Charles as a precise encapsulation of human reality from an holistic perspective. These five simple statements acknowledge our Sourceful power in responsibly creating our human experience. As such, they serve as powerful affirmations that can assist us in actualizing The Synchronicity Paradigm.

Principle One
I am Source, I am the Power.

There is only One. One Source Consciousness is the essence of all that is and is not. One Source Consciousness empowers all. As a human being, I am also this One Source Consciousness. Thus, in truth, I am Source, I am the Power.

Principle Two
I create my creation.

One Source Consciousness creates the creation. The creator is not different from the creation. There is only One. All is but the play of One Consciousness. I am Source. All is Source. Thus, as Source, I create my creation.

Principle Three
I am responsible for my creation.

One Source Consciousness creates the creation which is itself. Source is responsible for its creation because there is no one else. As Source, I am responsible for my creation.

Principle Four
I can change my creation.

There is only One Source Consciousness. The creation is the diversification of the creator, yet both are the same One. Creation is the play of the creator constantly changing the experience of itself. Thus, as Source, I consistently change my creation.

Principle Five
I am one and free.

The One and Only is only ever One. There is nothing in addition to it. It is independent and free. As The One and Only, I am One and free.

Actualizing the Synchronicity Paradigm

The Synchronicity Paradigm is based on The Synchronicity Holistic Cosmology of Reality, which has as its foundation, One Source Consciousness.   In its primary intention to fully be itself, One Source Consciousness creates The Relative Field, through which it can first become itself by experiencing what it is not..... diversity in relation to unity.   Thus, The Relative Field of Experience, from subtle to dense, is inherently imbalanced to the negative polarity by virtue of its expression as diversity and form. When we consider human experience, which is primarily focused in the three densest dimensions of The Relative Field, in which there is maximum imbalance, the intention to experience wholeness must first address balance. As balance is created in any dimension, that dimension yields to the next subtler level of experience, which, in turn, can also be balanced. Thus, human experience is a progressive process of ever-increasing integrative wholeness. The key to wholeness is balance. The Synchronicity Paradigm is designed to actualize wholeness through balance. It is an holistic model which addresses balance on both the interior and exterior levels, resulting in wholeness and fulfillment in human experience.

Synchronicity Holodynamic Technology

Synchronicity Holodynamic vibrational entrainment technology was created by Master Charles and is at the basis of all Synchronicity products and programs.   It entrains balance with technological precision in each dimension of the multi-dimensional human form. This can be observed in the brain with a computerized Brain Monitor.   Relative imbalance, or brain hemispheric lateralization, yields to relative balance or brain hemispheric synchrony. This vibrational entrainment technology is engineered onto every Synchronicity soundtrack at the audible/inaudible threshold, so the listener may not even be aware of its presence except through its effect.

On the interior, subjective level, Synchronicity Holodynamic Technology is included in all Synchronicity Contemporary Meditation Soundtracks. On the objective, environmental level, Synchronicity Holodynamic Technology, as used in The Harmonic Coherence Soundtrack, harmonizes and balances the chaotic environmental energies that surround us in our modern, technology-based world including radio, television and microwaves, atmospheric pollution and rapidly increasing population density, thus allowing us to more easily and efficiently experience balanced, holistic awareness.

Synchronicity Contemporary Meditation

Since the dawn of human experience on this planet, wholeness has been acknowledged as the basis of fulfillment. As wholeness is in proportion to balance, meditation, as a technology of balance, is a primary means to create wholeness and fulfillment in human experience.

The Synchronicity Holistic Model of Reality is based on One Source Consciousness as the foundation of a multi-dimensional field of relative experience, which is increasingly imbalanced to the negative polarity as it progresses from subtle to dense. In the three densest dimensions of The Relative Field, where human experience is primarily focused, imbalance is at a maximum. Thus, human beings endeavoring to create balance must begin at the level of maximum imbalance.

Additionally, when we endeavor to create balance through meditation, we must take into consideration the world in which we are living today. The world of today is not the same as the world of five thousand years ago, when meditation first evolved. Today's world is energetically far more complex and impactful than in ancient times. Modern technology has yielded many benefits, but has also created a vast network of energies that are imbalancing in relation to our own. From the electrical wiring in our homes and offices, to the TV, radio and microwaves that literally bombard us twenty-four hours a day, to the ever-increasing pollution and change in our oxygenation rate, to the incalculable impact of an exploding world population density with its stress and conflict, we are living in unprecedented times of energetic environmental challenges. Science recognizes the negative impact that these chaotic energies have on our ability to maintain balance. Thus, we are under constant stress in endeavoring to remain balanced in an imbalanced world.

All Synchronicity Contemporary Meditation soundtracks include Holodynamic technology which entrains whole-brain synchrony in far less time and with far less effort than traditional "low-tech" meditative techniques. Additionally, Synchronicity Contemporary Meditation Soundtracks are designed to harmonize and balance the chaotic environmental energies that surround us in our modern, technology-based world including radio, television and microwaves, atmospheric pollution and rapidly increasing population density.

In all, Synchronicity Contemporary Meditation Soundtracks deliver easy access to states of awareness traditionally achieved only with many years of disciplined practice. They may be used alone or in conjunction with any other meditation techniques you may presently employ.

Synchronicity Conscious Living Integrative Lifestyle

Synchronicity Conscious Living Integrative Lifestyle is designed to actualize The Synchronicity Paradigm on both the interior, subjective as well as exterior, objective levels of experience. Its primary focus is balance and it addresses every dimension of multi-dimensional human experience from dense to subtle.

In its interior, subjective aspect, Synchronicity Conscious Living Integrative Lifestyle addresses balance through a daily contemplative science practice of Synchronicity Contemporary Meditation. While meditation is a primary technology of balance, it cannot, on its own, actualize balance as a constant in human experience. The actualization of an integrative wholeness requires that we address balance on every dimension of human experience. Thus, Synchronicity Conscious Living Integrative Lifestyle includes a wide variety of tools and techniques designed to create balance on the physical, emotional, mental and environmental levels.

To create balance on the physical dimension, Synchronicity Conscious Living Integrative Lifestyle addresses diet and exercise as the primary means to create biochemical balance. A nutritionally balanced diet, such as The Zone Diet, by Dr. Barry Sears, is a key component in creating physical balance. The Zone Diet is recommended by Master Charles and is served on a daily basis at The Synchronicity Sanctuary as well as during all Synchronicity

Retreats. Additionally, aerobic exercise is another important component of Synchronicity Conscious Living Integrative Lifestyle that is a regular part of the daily schedule at Synchronicity Sanctuary, and is recommended by Master Charles for all Synchronicity Associates.

On the emotional dimension, Synchronicity Conscious Living Integrative Lifestyle addresses balance by bringing awareness to our feelings. To create balance in the emotional dimension, we consciously flow positive feelings throughout the day to balance the dominant negative polarity. Biochemical balance in the physical dimension through diet and exercise also supports hormonal balance in the emotional dimension. Additionally, we utilize the Heart-Wave Response, a simple technique which, once learned, can be used anytime to bring balance and coherence to the emotional dimension.

On the mental dimension, Conscious Living Integrative Lifestyle addresses balance by bringing awareness to our thinking. To create balance in the mental dimension, we consciously direct our mind to affirmative, positive thinking throughout the day to balance the dominant negative polarity. Biochemical and hormonal balance in the physical and emotional dimensions also supports neurochemical balance in the mental dimension.

On the environmental level, Conscious Living Integrative Lifestyle addresses balance through The Harmonic Coherence Soundtrack which harmonizes the energetic pollution that impacts us as a result of modern technology.

In all, Synchronicity Conscious Living Integrative Lifestyle is designed to actualize The Synchronicity Paradigm, bringing wholeness and fulfillment to human experience.

Part Four

The Recognitions Program

Sourceful awareness is blissful.
I am Source..... I am aware..... I am blissful.

The Synchronicity Recognitions Program

The Synchronicity Recognitions Program is Synchronicity Foundation's flagship, in-home, daily Contemporary Meditation course. Created by Master Charles in 1983 and continually refined and updated, The Recognitions Program is an integral part of Synchronicity Conscious Living Integrative Lifestyle. It is designed to actualize The Synchronicity Paradigm which includes Synchronicity Contemporary Meditation and Synchronicity Conscious Living Integrative Lifestyle and is based on The Synchronicity Holistic Model of Reality.

For nearly twenty years, The Recognitions Program has actualized the cutting edge of The Synchronicity Experience - Integrative Wholeness and Unity Consciousness - in the lives of its participants. This powerful transformational program utilizes Synchronicity Holodynamic vibrational entrainment technology in the delta range to deliver a precision experience of balance and resultant multi-dimensional consciousness awareness.

While the word "Recognitions" has its roots in ancient languages such as Latin and Sanskrit, in contemporary terms we may understand it as follows: Meditation is the foremost balancing technique in human experience. Balance is the foundation for experiencing holistic states of multi-dimensional awareness. As awareness expands, integrative wholeness and unity consciousness become increasingly dominant in our experience. Such subtle states of awareness have been classically delineated in terms of "consciousness in the recognition of itself".

Thus, The Recognitions Program is so named in acknowledgment of its experiential context. The delta-level technology it incorporates is designed to deliver the subtlest states of meditative awareness in which there is the experiential recognition of oneself as Source. With regular daily practice of The Recognitions Program, we progressively experience ever-increasing constancy in holistic Source Consciousness awareness, which is the basis for life lived in fulfillment.

As the basis of Synchronicity Conscious Living Integrative Lifestyle, The Recognitions Program is designed to actualize both the interior, subjective as well as the exterior, objective aspects of The Synchronicity Paradigm when used on a daily basis. It includes a multi-phased, progressive experience of precision meditation as its interior, subjective aspect. Additionally, The Recognitions Program addresses integrative wholeness in its exterior, objective dimension through regular facilitation with specially trained Recognition Program facilitators who have many years of experience with Synchronicity Contemporary Meditation and Conscious Living Integrative Lifestyle. Such regular facilitation is an essential part of The Recognitions Program, as it provides an opportunity for interactive dialogue and validation of experience not otherwise possible on one's own. The resultant clarity serves to further enhance balance and holistic awareness throughout each Phase of The Recognitions Program. Also, a wide range of supporting tools and technologies is recommended in relation to each Phase of The Recognitions Program to support integrative wholeness twenty-four hours a day.

Thus, The Recognitions Program fulfills the intention of its originator to actualize an integrative wholeness, comprising both the interior, subjective and the exterior, objective levels of human experience. It is designed for those committed individuals whose intention is to actualize an integrative wholeness in their daily life experience.

The Synchronicity Recognitions Program Retreats and Services

Certain Synchronicity Experience Retreats and Services are available exclusively to Recognitions Program participants. They are delineated as follows:

The Synchronicity Inner Network

The Synchronicity Inner Network is an interactive, experiential forum which connects Recognitions Program Associates with Master Charles and Synchronicity Sanctuary via the internet. Inner Network participants receive daily e-mail articles from Master Charles and a team of Synchronicity staff members, which address balance and holistic experience in relation to each dimension of The Synchronicity Holistic Model of Reality. Thus, balance is addressed in The Primary Trinity of physical, emotional and mental dimensions as well as the subtle dimensions that exist beyond the mind.

Inner Network participants are invited to share their experiences and questions in relation to each day's postings and the responses are then shared with everyone. In this way, a sense of conscious community is maintained which supports each Inner Network participant and significantly enriches their experience of integrative wholeness.

The Personal Mentoring Program

To experience excellence in any aspect of life, human beings have traditionally sought the guidance of a Mentor: an individual whose excellence is self-evident. Within The Synchronicity Experience, the role of the Mentor is considered invaluable in actualizing an ever-increasing integrative wholeness.

Personal Mentoring with Master Charles is a monthly consultation program, offered either in person or via telephone, that in addition to precision guidance in Contemporary Meditation and Conscious Living, includes home assignments, reference materials and much more. It is a rare opportunity to receive mentoring from one with masterful experience and the brilliance of conscious clarity that offers assistance in a succinct, practical and precise manner. There are two contexts of participation as follows:

Facilitated Mentoring with Master Charles

In this context, Master Charles supervises his team of specially trained facilitators to work directly with you. You will be assigned one of these facilitators with whom you will create an initial assessment of your meditative and conscious living experience, including areas of fulfillment as well as concern. Once per month, your facilitator will present your experience to Master Charles and relay his mentoring responses, insights and assignments directly to you. This is a progressive experience throughout the duration of your Recognitions Phase in which you will receive ongoing feedback to fine-tune your meditation practice and gain a more precise understanding of your conscious living experience. You may also elect to continue as you journey through the subsequent Recognitions Phases. This context requires Recognitions Phase duration commitment (three months), regular, daily practice of The Recognitions Program and participation in at least one Mastery Program per year.

Direct Mentoring with Master Charles

In this context, you consult directly with Master Charles, either in person or via telephone, once per month. Since only a specific number of spaces are available, individuals will be accepted on a first come, first served basis. This is a rare opportunity to receive direct mentoring from someone such as Master Charles. This context requires a six-month commitment, regular daily practice of The Recognitions Program and participation in at least two Mastery Programs per year.

The testimonials of both Direct and Facilitated Mentoring participants, confirms the extraordinary benefits of this unique Personal Mentoring Program.

The Contemporary Energetic Transmission

Beyond a Conscious Living Integrative Lifestyle and a daily Contemporary Meditation practice, The Mentor and Master of Meditation, as delineated in The Synchronicity Paradigm, expresses a state of integrative wholeness or unity consciousness and is capable of transmitting that Sourceful energetic vibration directly to the individual, catalyzing a proportional magnitude of expanded awareness and multi-dimensional wholeness. This is the time-honored and sought after experience of mystical empowerment, available only in relation to those rare human beings in whom unity consciousness and wholeness are a constant living reality.

As with Synchronicity Contemporary Meditation, Master Charles has applied precision technology to this ancient tradition, resulting in The High-Tech Empowerment, a one-on-one experience of energetic transmission. The High-Tech Empowerment has been available for many years at Synchronicity Sanctuary, but because of the need to be physically present, the availability of The High-Tech Empowerment has been limited only to Synchronicity Retreat participants.

The Contemporary Energetic Transmission is a cutting-edge application of The Synchronicity Experience, combining Master Charles' energetic transmission with an instantaneous delivery system based on precision computerized broadcasting technology. This subtle, energetically-based broadcasting technology extrapolates a unique energy pattern or signature from the recipient's hair or fingernail sample. This information is encoded and provides the individual's "Holographic Address", which is then used to precisely target the broadcast transmission. Thus, the experience of Master Charles' Sourceful energetic transmission is delivered to any individual, anywhere in the world without regard to distance. The experiential validation of Synchronicity associates world-wide is testimony to its authenticity and Sourceful power.

This is the contemporization of the ancient and time-honored experience of enlightening empowerment. It is Master Charles' particular genius..... the use of modern, empirical technology to deliver a precision transformational experience. Created by Master Charles, it is unique to Synchronicity Foundation. It is available only to Recognition Program Associates on a weekly or monthly subscription basis through Synchronicity Foundation.

The Synchronicity Four Seasons Mastery Program
With Master Charles

This week-long Synchronicity Experience Retreat is offered four times each year at The Synchronicity Sanctuary. It is exclusive to Recognitions Program participants. A detailed delineation of this program is included in the Retreat section.

The Synchronicity Empowerment Weekend Retreat
With Master Charles

This weekend Synchronicity Experience Retreat is offered several times each year at The Synchronicity Sanctuary. It is exclusive to Recognitions Program participants. A detailed delineation of this program is included in the Retreat section.

****

Part Five

*Synchronicity Contemporary
Meditation.....
A Comparison Study
How to Use
the Enclosed CD*

In meditation, I watch myself. Thoughts..... feelings..... colors..... lights..... I am amazed at the forms of myself. I am the One and Only.

Accelerated Transformation Through Contemporary Meditation

After years of research into the brain-wave patterns of regular users of Synchronicity Contemporary Meditation technology, we have developed the following study comparing the effects of Synchronicity Contemporary Meditation with traditional meditative systems: *A Comparison Study of Synchronicity Contemporary Meditators With Zen Monk Meditators.*

Introduction

One of the principal differences between Synchronicity Contemporary Meditation and traditional, orthodox (low-tech) systems of meditation is the speed with which measurable changes occur in one's state of awareness. This has been confirmed by measurement of the brain-wave patterns produced by regular users of Synchronicity Contemporary Meditation over a seven-year period. These were then compared to the measurements produced by those using traditional meditative systems.

There are a number of documented cases where groups of meditators using classical methods of meditation were measured. The most notable are the measurements made on the Dalai Lama's attendants (roughly twenty monks), during the early seventies, and more recently, those reported by Tomio Hirai, in the book *Zen Meditation and Psychotherapy*, in which forty Zen monks were studied and measured.

It should be noted that these studies represent the very best results that can be expected from the classical meditative disciplines, as these individuals were totally immersed in the contemplative lifestyle. Even those who are resident at The Synchronicity Sanctuary do not have the fully structured, meditative lifestyle of cloistered monks. Further, most participants in The Synchronicity Recognitions Program (the correspondence course which utilizes Synchronicity Contemporary Meditation on a daily basis), live everyday lives in cities, working normal jobs, raising families and enduring the distractions which those experiences engender..... not at all what one would define as a contemplative lifestyle.

The results of the two studies of classical meditators were basically the same. Novices (their term), were considered to be those who had five years or less meditative experience. These individuals consistently produced mid to high-frequency alpha waves (10 to 12 Hz.). Moderately experienced meditators (ten to twenty years experience) continually produced low frequency alpha (7 to 9 Hz.), the actual frequency being lower as experience increased. Very experienced meditators, those with twenty to forty years experience, consistently produced theta frequencies in the 5 to 6 Hz. range. An interesting aside is that the experimenters made no mention of the other bands of frequencies. Delta (0.5 to 3.5 Hz.), has long been considered to be the most notable sign of an expanded state of awareness typical of enlightening beings. Alpha (7 to 13 Hz.) is considered necessary for attentive focus, and beta (14 to 25 Hz.) is necessary to retain conscious awareness. In the absence of beta and alpha, the presence of delta indicates Stage One sleep.

The reason the other frequencies are not mentioned in these studies is probably due to the fact that the researchers used traditional electroencephalographs (EEG's) for their measurements. The wave forms from EEG's are characterized by being mostly alpha, or primarily theta, or REM, or sleep spindles, etc. This is because the data from EEG's are complex super-impositions of frequencies which are difficult to decompose into more fundamental constituents. Thus, they cannot say much about specific frequencies, other than the dominant ones.

Similar research by C.M. Cade and N. Coxhead (The Awakened Mind. Element Books Ltd, Longmead, Shaftesbury, Dorset, Eng., 1989) involved an instrument called the mind mirror, which used analog filters to transform the data to the frequency domain so that brain-wave frequencies could be observed instead of the trains of composite amplitudes characteristic of the EEG. One of the results of their measurements was a delineation of the profile of frequencies present for various states of awareness. Their state V, which they call the "Awakened Mind," reflecting the state of enlightening awareness, is comprised of beta (typically from 15 to 17 Hz.), along with a noticeable peak in alpha (in the 7-8 Hz. region), a theta bulge (in the 5-6 Hz. area), and expanding delta (i.e. increasing in amplitude as the frequency approaches zero). Many Synchronicity Recognitions Program meditators exhibit this state V response on the Brain Monitor, which also displays data in the frequency amplitude domain.

Results

Our extensive research has shown that as they begin The Recognitions Program, most people produce alpha at 11 or 12 Hz. This is consistent with patterns demonstrated by novice Buddhist monks. As individuals move through The Recognitions Program, however, their brain-wave patterns shift, the alpha peaks becoming lower in frequency, larger in amplitude and more persistent in time. As they acquire more experience, we see more theta and developing delta. Symmetry improves throughout, although left to right coherence, which we call synchrony factor, often varies as a function of the moment. It reflects the bliss as well as the clearing often experienced by a meditator and is a measure of the equilibration experienced at the time of the measurement.

The accompanying Brain Monitor results are typical of our findings. These scans include both residents of The Synchronicity Sanctuary and non-resident participants in The Recognitions Program. The major point of interest is that none of these meditators has more than seven years experience with Synchronicity vibrational entrainment technology - most of them less than that - yet they continually demonstrated brain-wave patterns consistent with advanced meditators (twenty years or more experience) in the Buddhist monk studies. These findings empirically validate the assertion first advanced by Master Charles in The Synchronicity Paradigm in 1983, that Synchronicity Contemporary Meditation represents a four-fold acceleration factor over classical methods of meditation. The following data is presented for purposes of comparison of Synchronicity meditators with the Buddhist monk studies in terms of consistency of measured dominant brain-wave frequencies in relation to years of meditative experience.

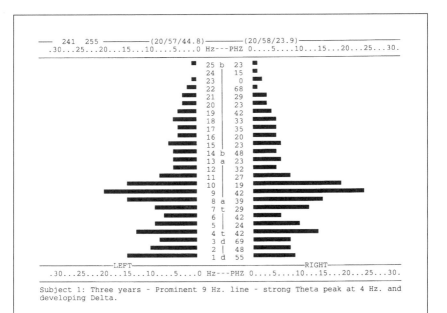

```
 ——  241  255 ——————(20/57/44.8)——————(20/58/23.9)——————————
 .30...25...20...15...10....5....0 Hz---PHZ 0....5....10...15...20...25...30.
                                  ■   25 b  23  ■
                                      24    15
                                      23 |   0
                                      22    68  ■
                                      21    29
                                      20    23
                                      19    42
                                      18    33
                                      17    35
                                      16    20
                                      15 |  23
                                      14 b  48
                                      13 a  23
                                      12 |  32
                                      11    27
                                      10    19
                                       9 |  42
                                       8 a  39
                                       7 t  29
                                       6 |  42
                                       5 |  24
                                       4 t  42
                                       3 d  69
                                       2 |  48
                                       1 d  55
 —————————————————LEFT—————————————                    ——RIGHT———
 .30...25...20...15...10....5....0 Hz---PHZ 0....5....10...15...20...25...30.
```

Subject 1: Three years - Prominent 9 Hz. line - strong Theta peak at 4 Hz. and developing Delta.

```
 ——  496  510 ——————( 0/23/46.7)——————( 0/24/19.5)——————————
 .30...25...20...15...10....5....0 Hz---PHZ 0....5....10...15...20...25...30.
                                  ■   25 b   0  ■
                                      24     0  ■
                                      23 |  45
                                      22    39
                                      21    51
                                      20    70
                                      19 |  77
                                      18    60
                                      17    51
                                      16    83
                                      15 |  83
                                      14 b  30
                                      13 a  34
                                      12 |  45
                                      11    69
                                      10    58
                                       9 |  68
                                       8 a  15
                                       7 t  19
                                       6 |  35
                                       5 |  30
                                       4 t  33
                                       3 d  48
                                       2 |  45
                                       1 d  39
 —————————————————LEFT—————————————                    ——RIGHT———
 .30...25...20...15...10....5....0 Hz---PHZ 0....5....10...15...20...25...30.
```

Subject 2: Four years - Strong Alpha at 8 Hz. - excellent Theta peak at 5 Hz. with developing Delta.

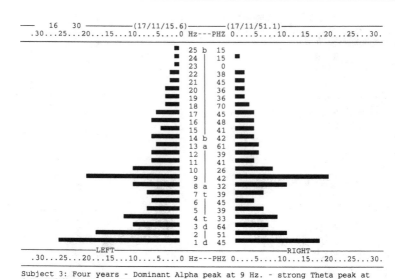

Subject 3: Four years - Dominant Alpha peak at 9 Hz. - strong Theta peak at 4 Hz. with excellent Delta.

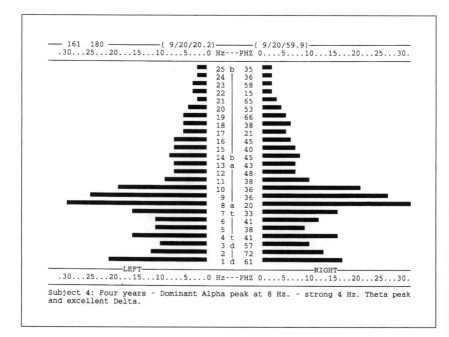

Subject 4: Four years - Dominant Alpha peak at 8 Hz. - strong 4 Hz. Theta peak and excellent Delta.

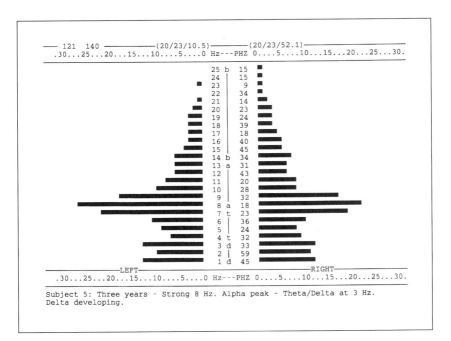

```
—— 121  140 ————————(20/23/10.5)————(20/23/52.1)———————
.30...25...20...15...10....5....0 Hz---PHZ 0....5....10...15...20...25...30.
                                    25 b 15
                                    24 | 15
                                    23   9
                                    22   34
                                    21   14
                                    20   23
                                    19   24
                                    18   39
                                    17   18
                                    16   40
                                    15 | 45
                                    14 b 34
                                    13 a 31
                                    12 | 43
                                    11   20
                                    10 | 28
                                     9 | 32
                                     8 a 18
                                     7 t 23
                                     6 | 36
                                     5 | 24
                                     4 t 32
                                     3 d 33
                                     2 | 59
                                     1 d 45
————————————LEFT————————————————————————RIGHT————
.30...25...20...15...10....5....0 Hz---PHZ 0....5....10...15...20...25...30.
```

Subject 5: Three years - Strong 8 Hz. Alpha peak - Theta/Delta at 3 Hz. Delta developing.

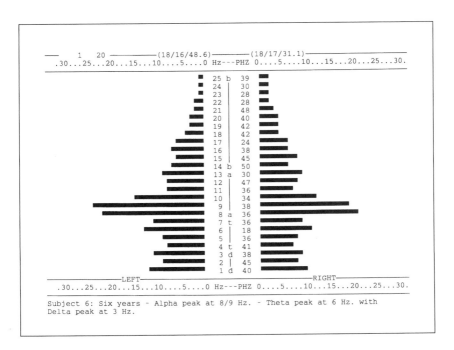

```
——  1  20 ————————(18/16/48.6)————————(18/17/31.1)————————
.30...25...20...15...10....5....0 Hz---PHZ 0....5....10...15...20...25...30.
                                    25 b 39
                                    24 | 30
                                    23   28
                                    22   28
                                    21   48
                                    20   40
                                    19   42
                                    18   42
                                    17   24
                                    16   38
                                    15 | 45
                                    14 b 50
                                    13 a 30
                                    12 | 47
                                    11   36
                                    10 | 34
                                     9 | 38
                                     8 a 36
                                     7 t 36
                                     6 | 18
                                     5 | 36
                                     4 t 41
                                     3 d 38
                                     2 | 45
                                     1 d 40
————————————LEFT————————————————————————RIGHT————
.30...25...20...15...10....5....0 Hz---PHZ 0....5....10...15...20...25...30.
```

Subject 6: Six years - Alpha peak at 8/9 Hz. - Theta peak at 6 Hz. with Delta peak at 3 Hz.

Brain Waves and Meditation

What, specifically, do the terms beta, alpha, theta, and delta mean for the contemporary meditator? What type of changes actually occur in brain-wave frequencies as one progressively experiences a more holistic awareness? Current technology, including the one-of-a-kind "Brain Monitor" developed by Synchronicity Foundation's research team, enables us to answer these questions with precision.

In this section we will consider how Synchronicity's empirical vibrational entrainment technology effects the development of hemispheric synchronization and whole-brain function, resulting in a transformational experience which unfolds from alpha through delta, from light relaxation to deep transcendental meditation.

Alpha

When brain-wave activity is focused primarily within the 8-13 Hz. (cycles per second) range, one experiences what is termed an "alpha" state of awareness. Alpha brain-waves are produced in most people when they concentrate or focus the mind, or relax by sitting or reclining with their eyes closed. Alpha brain-waves are very often produced in bursts (trains of waves) or pulses (single waves), but some people, and especially Synchronicity Contemporary meditators, tend to produce continuous trains of alpha waves. When your brain is producing alpha frequencies, you experience a pleasant, comfortable, mildly relaxed yet wakeful state of awareness.

This experience represents a relatively stress-free and euphoric state of being. The general understanding is that the more that alpha is produced in ordinary states of awareness, the easier it is to access deeper meditative states.

Practically speaking, individuals such as artists or photographers, who more often than usual, use the visual and spatial abilities characteristic of the right-brain, seem to produce alpha more easily than linear, left-brain thinkers. In the same way, experienced Synchronicity Contemporary meditators, who have repetitively patterned and become familiar with alpha brain-wave production, can more easily produce alpha frequencies.

In fact, by looking at an individual's alpha brain-wave production, it is possible to determine not only whether the person is a meditator, but also the length of time the individual has been practicing meditation. Beginning meditators tend to produce alpha in the 10 to 12 Hz. range. As meditative experience deepens, so does the dominant frequency at which alpha is produced. Therefore, we find that meditators with ten plus years of experience consistently produce low frequency alpha in the region of 7 to 9 Hz.

Theta

Theta brain-waves are produced in the frequency range from 3.5-7 Hz., which are more decelerated brain waves than alpha. Like alpha, theta is characterized by a blissful sense of well-being. However, in theta, the experience of holistic awareness increases. Theta represents the synchronized state of awareness in which creativity and imagery predominate. Experienced meditators are accustomed to a wide variety of "inner" images and visions, and these images do indeed seem to correlate with increased theta activity.

Delta

Delta brain waves are traditionally associated with deep sleep and are the slowest of the brain waves, occurring from 0-3.5 Hertz. Usually, only the most advanced meditators can remain conscious while producing delta brain waves. The experiences leading to the threshold of mental dimension transcendence occur in the deepest levels of the delta brain-wave frequencies.

Our research has shown that with regular use of The Synchronicity Recognitions Program, which utilizes Synchronicity delta-level, vibrational entrainment technology, contemporary meditators develop constancy in the production of delta brain-waves. Thus, after only a few years of regular usage, Synchronicity Contemporary meditators produce brain-wave patterns equal to those individuals who have spent a lifetime of practice using traditional methods.

When and Where to Meditate

Along with a clear understanding of The Synchronicity Paradigm, let us now address some of the more practical aspects of Synchronicity Contemporary Meditation. The benefits of meditation accrue through regular, daily practice. Depending upon your schedule, twenty or thirty minutes, up to an hour or more per day is considered an average range of meditation practice for most people. Some meditators prefer one longer sitting of perhaps an hour or more, while for others, meditating twice a day for a shorter duration works better. You will know, based upon your experience, what is best for you.

Meditation is most productive when practiced in the morning, shortly after arising, when the mind and body are rested and alert. Aerobic exercise is recommended immediately prior to meditation in order to bring the physical body to a state of balance, thus supporting you in your intention to meditate. Choose a quiet, comfortable area for meditation where you will not be disturbed. Sit in an upright position, either in a chair or on the floor. Then put on stereo headphones, begin the soundtrack, and listen; the technology will do the rest.

If your experience during meditation is something other than a quiet mind, peacefully aware..... do not be alarmed..... or surprised. An upsurge of thinking during this time is commonly experienced by meditators. Just observe what is happening in your experience and make no judgments about what occurs. As you begin to experience a more holistic awareness, the limiting "data" of the mind is simply rising to the level of conscious awareness to be released as part of the clearing process. Whenever you become aware that you have been absorbed in thinking, simply return to the wakeful observation of your experience. Meditation happens whenever there is awareness.

If you find that you "go out" during meditation, you may not be asleep in the way you normally understand it. Expanded states of awareness are sometimes experienced as visionary or dreamlike states, often of a very insightful or creative nature. During such times, the meditator is neither fully awake nor asleep in the conventional sense. Rather, what is experienced is a very subtle state of awareness which may not be consciously cognized. Another expression of expanded awareness is the experience of heaviness or intoxication. The groggy feeling that you may experience initially is simply the dense physical body's response to the subtle energies released through meditation. You will become clearer as this state is integrated. Accept it as evidence, yet again, that your meditation is working.

How to Use the Enclosed CD

The enclosed CD is a sixty-minute Synchronicity Contemporary Meditation Soundtrack which includes Synchronicity Holodynamic vibrational entrainment technology in the theta range. It is designed to deliver The Synchronicity Experience - whole-brain synchrony and holistic awareness though balance. It is included with the intention of allowing you, the reader, to be able to experience precision, Synchronicity Contemporary Meditation for yourself.

To enjoy a personal meditative experience with this Synchronicity Contemporary Meditation Soundtrack, we recommend using a standard component or portable CD player with stereo headphones. Sit comfortably with closed eyes and adjust the volume to a comfortable listening level as you begin. As the soundtrack plays, The Synchronicity Holodynamic technology embedded within the music, balances the brain hemispheres and entrains whole brain synchrony. While you are listening, the meditative experience will progress and the relaxed, wakeful and expanded state of awareness characteristic of precision meditation will continue. If you notice that you are thinking, simply shift your attention back to the soundtrack.

You may meditate for twenty or thirty minutes, up to a full hour as you wish. However long you meditate, it is recommended that you conclude with a few minutes of silent meditation (without the soundtrack), as a means of integrating your experience and transitioning smoothly back into normal activity.

Part Six

Synchronicity Retreats, Products and Services

Life is a progressive process of ever-increasing integrative wholeness. In every way..... every day..... I am more than I have ever been.

The Synchronicity Experience
Contemporary Meditation
Conscious Living Integrative Lifestyle
Retreats, Products and Services

Retreats

The Synchronicity Paradigm is designed to actualize The Synchronicity Holistic Cosmology of Reality and deliver the experience of wholeness through balance that is the basis of human fulfillment. The Synchronicity Paradigm is experientially validated through Synchronicity Contemporary Meditation and Synchronicity Conscious Living Integrative Lifestyle.

While it is quite possible and practical to experience an ever-increasing integrative wholeness in the midst of a normal, daily lifestyle, many individuals endeavor to revitalize and deepen their experience by periodically attending retreat programs at Synchronicity Sanctuary. In this context, The Synchronicity

Experience is available in its most impactful form, as every Synchronicity Retreat includes the opportunity to experience the Sourceful energetic of Master Charles as well as the Conscious Living Integrative Lifestyle and Contemporary form of Meditation that he created.

In addition, The Synchronicity Sanctuary is an holistic environment that is consistently maintained in a state of balance through the conscious intention that is its basis. This Sourceful, nurturing environment supports the experience of multi-dimensional, holistic awareness far beyond what is normally available on one's own. Thus, it is commonly observed that those who attend Synchronicity Retreats move beyond their usual level of experience to more expanded states of holistic awareness.

Synchronicity Retreats are offered in several formats to accommodate a variety of experience as follows:

The Synchronicity Four Seasons Mastery Program

As nature renews itself four times each year, The Synchronicity Four Seasons Mastery Program is offered in each season to provide an opportunity for an holistic experience of renewal and balance. This week-long experience of Synchronicity Contemporary Meditation and Conscious Living Integrative Lifestyle is focused on daily interactive programs with Master Charles during which the conscious living meditative journey is explored in great depth and subtlety.

In addition, there is a full schedule of Conscious Living Integrative Lifestyle experience including daily sessions of Synchronicity

Contemporary Meditation utilizing the deepest levels of Synchronicity Holodynamic technology, group meetings in which participants explore questions and insights in relation to their meditative experience, and a wide variety of Integrative Protocols which assist in the process of balancing and rejuvenation.

The Four Seasons Mastery Program is offered in February, May, August and October at Synchronicity Sanctuary in central Virginia and is open to Recognitions Program associates. A current retreat program calendar is available on our web-site: www.synchronicity.org.

The Synchronicity Experience Introductory Retreat
Welcome to Our World

The Synchronicity Experience Introductory Retreat is an opportunity for those who are new to Synchronicity to experience Master Charles and The Synchronicity Sanctuary. The theme for the program is: *An Introduction to Synchronicity Contemporary Meditation and Conscious Living as Created by Master Charles*, with a focus on The Synchronicity Paradigm and the mechanics and benefits of Conscious Living and Contemporary Meditation as a regular daily experience of balance, wholeness and awareness expansion.

This in-residence, four-day retreat includes The High-Tech Empowerment with Master Charles, an experience of harmonic coherence and unity consciousness. The High-Tech Empowerment is the contemporization of the ancient and time-honored experience of energetic transmission from an authentic mystic and meditation master. In addition, those attendees not yet in The Recognitions Program will receive Recognitions - One as part of their program materials, along with guidance in using The Recognitions Program on a daily basis.

"Welcome to Our World" Introductory Retreats are scheduled regularly throughout the year and are open to all meditators, both new and experienced.

Synchronicity Empowerment Weekend Retreat

The Synchronicity Empowerment Retreat is an in-residence weekend retreat which includes an evening program with Master Charles and The Synchronicity High-Tech Empowerment. The High-Tech Empowerment is a contemporized version of the ancient and time-honored experience of mystical transmission, utilizing precision Synchronicity technology created by Master Charles in combination with his individualized energetic transmission. Until now, The High-Tech Empowerment has been available only in the context of The Synchronicity Four Seasons Mastery Program. The Synchronicity Empowerment Retreat is offered on a bi-monthly basis throughout the year and is open to Recognitions Program Associates.

Products

Synchronicity Contemporary Meditation Soundtracks include Synchronicity Holodynamic vibrational entrainment technology and are available in two formats, each addressing a specific level of meditative experience, for both individual meditation and environmental balance. Synchronicity Alpha Soundtracks entrain balanced brain wave frequencies in the 8 -14 Hz. range and are designed for a light, balancing meditative experience which supports mental clarity and focus. Alpha soundtracks are an excellent introduction to Synchronicity Contemporary Meditation and may be used either with headphones for personal meditation or with speakers to enhance any environment.

Synchronicity Theta Soundtracks entrain balanced brain-wave frequencies in 3.5 - 7 Hz. range and are designed for a medium-level meditation experience which supports more expanded states of awareness. Theta is considered to be the range in which creative inspiration and insight is more easily accessible. Synchronicity Theta Soundtracks may also be used either with headphones for personal meditation or with speakers to enhance any environment.

Synchronicity Alpha and Theta Soundtracks are available in both CD and cassette formats and may be sampled on our web-site: www.synchronicity.org.

Synchronicity Sampler CD - a sixty-minute Synchronicity Sampler CD and information package is available through Synchronicity Foundation. The Sampler CD includes twelve - five minute samples from our most popular Synchronicity Alpha and Theta Soundtracks. Also included are printed materials on Synchronicity products, programs and services.

The Bliss of Freedom - A Contemporary Mystic's Enlightening Journey by Master Charles

Sooner or later, every sincere seeker of truth encounters the classic works of spiritual illumination as part of their own journey of inner exploration. To this select group of books must be added Master

Charles' contemporary spiritual autobiography, *The Bliss of Freedom*. This first-hand account of the full unfoldment of holistic awareness in the life of a modern Western mystic, is expressed with such clarity, that the mystical dimensions of human experience become understandable and applicable to our own lives. *The Bliss of Freedom* is a must read for anyone endeavoring to grasp the truth of what it means to be fully human.

Synchronicity Balance Blends

Synchronicity Balance Blends are formulated by M.C. Cannon (Master Charles), who has thoroughly explored the field of aroma as it relates to whole-brain function and meditative awareness.

Aroma is now understood to be a powerful means of creating balance and transforming awareness, as it rapidly accesses the deepest centers of the brain through the olfactory nerve which affects how we perceive and feel. Within moments, the appropriate scent can change anxiety to a peaceful state of relaxation, or bring focus and clarity whenever there is fatigue. Aroma can also be used to create balance in the two brain hemispheres thus creating an ideal inner environment for holistic awareness. Each Synchronicity Balance Blend is designed to deliver a soothing, peaceful ambience to any environment. They are the perfect balancing tools for enhancing meditation or any activity. There are nine unique Synchronicity Balance Blends, each containing only the highest quality pure essential oils without diluents, alcohol or synthetics.

Synchronicity Products

Synchronicity Contemporary Meditation Soundtracks

All Synchronicity Contemporary Meditation Soundtracks include Synchronicity Holodynamic vibrational entrainment technology and are available in two formats, alpha and theta..... each addressing a specific level of meditative experience, for both individual meditation and environmental balance. Benefits include: deep relaxation and experience of well-being, euphoria, increased creativity, clarity or insight, greater balance and focus in everyday life, improvements in overall health and balance, and access to holistic, multi-dimensional states of Sourceful awareness and unity consciousness.

Synchronicity Alpha Soundtracks

Synchronicity Alpha Soundtracks entrain balanced brain wave frequencies in the 8 -14 Hz. range and are designed for a light, balancing meditative experience which supports mental clarity and focus. Alpha soundtracks are an excellent introduction to Synchronicity Contemporary Meditation and may be used either with headphones for personal meditation or with speakers to enhance any environment. Following is a listing of our full range of alpha-level meditation soundtracks available in both CD and cassette tape format:

Welcome To My World

One of our most popular soundtracks, Welcome To My World is the first Synchronicity Soundtrack created by Master Charles. It is designed for both environmental, background music and light, relaxing meditation with stereo headphones. It features a soothing combination of Master Charles' voice with repetitive melody, guitar, synthesizer, veena and the gentle sound of a babbling brook.

This beautiful meditation soundtrack contains Synchronicity Holodynamic technology in the alpha range which entrains whole-brain synchrony and a precision alpha state of light meditation. When used with stereo headphones, it quickly delivers a relaxed, peaceful and balanced state of being.

Om - The Reverberation of Source

OM is an ancient Sanskrit word symbolizing the phenomenal energy vibration of Reality or what Master Charles calls Source. It has become a universal mantra, though its origin is Eastern. It is traditionally used as a meditative sound to still the mind and invoke inner peace and Sourceful awareness.

This beautiful meditation soundtrack features Master Charles' voice, synthesizer, veena and the meditative sound of the ocean. It also utilizes Synchronicity alpha level Holodynamic technology which enhances whole-brain synchrony and entrains a precision alpha state of light meditation. When used with stereo headphones, it quickly delivers a balanced, peaceful and harmonious state of being.

Om Mani Padme Hum

Om Mani Padme Hum is a mantra from the Buddhist tradition which means "The Supreme Reality (is the) lotus jewel of Oneness." It identifies the non-dual essence that is the One and Supreme Reality and acknowledges its expression within human experience.

This soundtrack features a tapestry of Master Charles' voice and voice chorus harmonics in repetitive melody, with the subtle background chorus of chanting monks with cymbals and is accompanied by veena, synthesizer and the environmental sound of the whispering wind. It also utilizes Synchronicity alpha level Holodynamic technology.

Om Namah Shivaya

Om Namah Shivaya is a Sanskrit mantra dating back at least five thousand years, which means "I bow to God." It is traditionally used as a prayer to invoke the Divine Presence within the heart.

This soundtrack features a very slow and subtle combination of Master Charles' voice and voice chorus harmonics in repetitive melody accompanied by veena, synthesizer, and the background sound of the gentle ocean. It also utilizes Synchronicity alpha level Holodynamic technology.

Synchronicity Theta Soundtracks

Synchronicity Theta soundtracks entrain balanced brain-wave frequencies in 3.5 - 7 Hz. range and are designed for a medium-level meditation experience which supports more expanded states of holistic awareness. Theta is considered to be the range in which creative inspiration and insight is more easily accessible. Synchronicity Theta Soundtracks may also be used either with headphones for personal meditation or with speakers to enhance any environment.

The Collaborations Series

The Collaborations Series is a unique collection of Synchronicity musical meditation soundtracks, each created by an internationally renowned artist in collaboration with Master Charles and Synchronicity Holodynamic vibrational entrainment technology in the theta range. They may be used with headphones for a deeply relaxing and soothing meditative experience, or with speakers to enhance any environment.

Collaborations - Echoes of Stillness

Our newest release in the Collaborations Series features internationally acclaimed recording artist Kamal with healing and soothing musical instrumentation in combination with Master Charles' Synchronicity Holodynamic technology in the theta range. Track One is entitled Stillness1 and Track Two is entitled Stillness 2. Each track is thirty minutes long.

Collaborations - Into the Moment

This album features the musical artistry of Steven Halpern, internationally acclaimed composer and sound healer, in combination with Master Charles and Synchronicity Holodynamic technology in the theta range. Track One is Into the Moment and Track Two is Beyond the Mind. Each track is thirty minutes long.

Collaborations - The Meditative Flute

This album features Riley Lee, Shakuhachi flute master, in combination with Master Charles and Synchronicity Holodynamic technology in the theta range. The Shakuhachi is a simple, traditional, Japanese bamboo flute whose tones are subtle and evoke the essence of meditative awareness in musical form. Track One is The Fullness of Emptiness and Track Two is Diversity in Unity. Each track is thirty minutes long.

The Sounds of Source

The Sounds of Source Series of Synchronicity Contemporary Meditation soundtracks is the slowest, most continually meditative music available. They may be used with headphones for a deeply relaxing meditative experience, or with speakers as a balancing, ambient background for massage, yoga, or any activity. Each soundtrack includes Synchronicity Holodynamic technology in the theta range. Each album includes two thirty minute tracks, ideal for uninterrupted, continuous meditation.

The Sounds of Source - Volume One

Sounds of Source - One features a lush orchestral score of sampled voice and strings in two tracks: Symphony of Stillness 1 and Symphony of Stillness 2.

The Sounds of Source - Volume Two

Sounds of Source - Two uses ambient sampled voice and instruments to produce a very spatial, other-worldly meditative experience. Track One is Sacred Silhouettes 1 and Track Two is Sacred Silhouettes 2.

The Sounds of Source - Volume Three

Sounds of Source - Three features flute, voice, whale songs and soothing ocean waves in two beautiful tracks entitled Return to Silence and Out of Emptiness.

The Sounds of Source - Volume Four

Sounds of Source - Four features the uplifting sounds of echoing flutes in two tracks entitled Peaceful Circumference and Luminous Ecstasy.

The Sounds of Source - Volume Five

Here is the latest in the Sounds of Source Series - this new soundtrack contains two thirty minute selections, Echoes of Eternity and Silent Spaces. Both feature a soothing combination of sampled voice and slow-moving, ethereal sound.

Time Off - The Fifteen Minute Meditator

Time Off - The Fifteen Minute Meditator is designed to be used anywhere - at work, home, school or on the go. Track one contains a bell-tone synthesizer soundtrack which entrains a deep theta - level meditation. For an extended thirty-minute meditation, continue with track two where the Synchronicity Holodynamic technology continues with the sounds of the gently rolling ocean surf. Available in both cassette and CD format for use with stereo headphones.

Song of the Ecstatic

In this unique soundtrack, Master Charles sings select verses from this ancient song in the original Sanskrit to classical accompaniment with contemporary sound enhancements. It is the meditative treatise of a legendary enlightening mystic expressing the joyful truth of the Oneness of all that is. A blissful, one-hour soundtrack that can be used either for meditation or environmental listening.

Harmonic Coherence

This unique soundtrack is specifically designed to create balance when used with speakers in any environment. The Synchronicity Holodynamic vibrational entrainment technology it includes, harmonizes and balances the chaotic energetic frequencies that result from electronic appliances, equipment and power sources that increasingly proliferate in our living and work spaces. These chaotic frequencies conflict with our own natural energy field, thus challenging us in our ability to remain balanced and whole.

The Harmonic Coherence Soundtrack features sixty minutes of special Synchronicity vibrational entrainment technology along with the soothing sound of ocean waves and is designed to be played as a continuous background in any environment.

Synchronicity Aromatherapy Products - Balance Blends

Synchronicity Balance Blends are a unique collection of nine pure essential oil blends designed to enhance well-being and support holistic awareness. They are formulated by Master Charles who has thoroughly explored the field of aroma as it relates to whole-brain function and meditative awareness. Each Synchronicity Balance Blend is designed to deliver a soothing, peaceful ambience to any environment. They are the perfect balancing tools for enhancing meditation or harmonizing any environment.

Synchronicity Balance Blends contain only the highest quality, pure essential oils, without diluents, alcohol or synthetics.

There are nine unique Synchronicity Balance Blends to choose from:

Transcendence - Contents: Juniper Berry, Peru Balsam and Vetiver.

Tranquility - Contents: Rosewood, Bergamot, Cedarwood and Sandalwood.

Quiescence - Contents: Spruce, Cistus and Clove.

Harmony - Contents: Peru Balsam, Ylang Ylang, Sandalwood and Tangerine.

Serenity - Contents: Cypress, Frankincense and Bergamot.

Equanimity - Contents: Peru Balsam, Bergamot, Lavender, Clary Sage and Ylang Ylang.

Simplicity - Contents: Palmarosa, Cistus, Sandalwood and Grapefruit.

Bliss - Contents: Roman Chamomile, Labdanum, Clary Sage and Sweet Orange.

Millennium - Contents: Roman Chamomile, Palmarosa, Rosewood, Sweet Orange, Grapefruit and Sandalwood.

Synchronicity Balance Blends are recommended for use in hand-blown, glass electric oil diffusers. Utilizing a silent electric air pump, oils are dispersed in the form of micro-droplets, sending a fine mist of fragrance into the air. Micro-droplets are negatively charged and have a purifying, vitalizing effect on the environment. These precision aroma generators are available through Synchronicity Foundation and are designed to be used with Synchronicity Balance Blends. Please inquire for prices and specifications.

Services

Peace of Mind Shop

The Peace of Mind Shop features a unique collection of conscious living accessories, gifts and specialty items chosen by Master Charles for their balancing and awareness-enhancing qualities. The Peace of Mind Collection includes the best of meditative music, aroma products, books, nutritional supplements, tools for health and well-being and much more. The Peace of Mind Shop is available on-line at: www.synchronicity.org. We also maintain a small retail outlet on The Synchronicity Sanctuary grounds. Please contact Synchronicity Sanctuary for more information on The Peace of Mind Shop including hours and new products.

Part Seven

Conclusion

Be aware. This is a Sourceful moment. There is only One.

Conclusion
The Twenty-Year Experiment Continues into the Millennium

The Synchronicity Paradigm, including Synchronicity Contemporary Meditation and Synchronicity Conscious Living Integrative Lifestyle, was created by Master Charles nearly twenty years ago. Since that time, we have had an opportunity to apply this model full-time on a daily basis within The Synchronicity Community at Synchronicity Sanctuary, in the Blue Ridge Mountains of central Virginia. In addition, we have an extended community of thousands of active participants in The Synchronicity Experience world-wide, who practice Synchronicity Contemporary Meditation on a daily basis and live a Conscious Living Integrative Lifestyle in the midst of their active lives.

While the history of human life on this planet is rich in conscious living and holistic human experience as documented in The Great Wisdom Traditions across many cultures and times, it is very rare to find such a context in these contemporary times. Thus, we can understand The Synchronicity Experience in terms of a twenty year experiment in which we can test the validity and effectiveness of this contemporary model.

What the Twenty-Year Experiment Validates

As delineated in The Synchronicity Paradigm, One Source Consciousness is the basis of a multi-dimensional reality from subtle to dense, including human experience. Master Charles originally postulated that a Conscious Living Integrative Lifestyle, including a daily practice of Synchronicity Contemporary Meditation along with a consistent focus on balance in each dimension of The Primary Trinity of mind, emotions and body, would result in the validation of this model of reality..... holistic awareness and fulfillment in human experience. Additionally, he asserted that a technological approach to such holistic experience would bring precision and acceleration to the process.

In nearly twenty years of ongoing exploration in this experiment, we have seen, time and time again, the validation of The Synchronicity Paradigm in the experience of those participating in it. When the practice of Synchronicity Contemporary Meditation is applied on a daily basis, along with Synchronicity Conscious Living Integrative Lifestyle and its tools and technologies of balance..... human transformation is the result. Fragmentation and a negative dominant, fear-based experience of life yields to balance, thus delivering the wholeness and fulfillment that is the hallmark of conscious living.

What The Twenty-Year Experiment Demonstrates

Firstly, in the Synchronicity Community, where The Synchronicity Paradigm has been consistently lived on a full-time basis, we have seen a constant demonstration of the effectiveness of this model in relation to human transformation. Imbalance in all dimensions of The Primary Trinity of body, emotions and mind is brought to balance with a constant emphasis on the non-dominant positive polarity. A balanced diet and daily exercise regime delivers vitality and well-being to the physical dimension. A consistent focus on flowing positive feeling and the regular use of techniques such as The Heart-Wave Response, delivers balance to the emotional dimension, resulting in contentment and fulfillment. Daily practice of Synchronicity Contemporary Meditation along with the use of positive affirmations and focusing techniques brings balance to the mental dimension, resulting in wakeful, peaceful clarity and a consistent flow of creative inspiration.

Secondly, in the extended family of Synchronicity participants, who comprise a worldwide community of many thousands of people, we observe a very compelling demonstration of the effectiveness of The Synchronicity Paradigm. While the challenges of living with balance in an imbalanced world are ever-increasing, the experiences of balanced, holistic awareness and integrative wholeness, even without the supportive environment of Synchronicity Sanctuary, are comparable in many cases to those of the full-time Synchronicity Community. Many Synchronicity participants demonstrate on a daily basis, the rare and classical experiences of holistic, multi-dimensional awareness that are well-documented in the classical writings of The Great Wisdom Traditions of human experience.

The Synchronicity Experience - Where We Are Today

As human experience is a progressive process of ever-increasing integrative wholeness, Synchronicity Foundation continues to evolve new ways and means to further contemporize and bring greater precision to the transformational process that is life itself. The opportunity to make The Synchronicity Experience available to greater numbers of individuals via the internet is a major impetus for creating new E-Programs and products. Ongoing advances in technology have made it possible for Synchronicity participants world-wide to interact with Master Charles and Synchronicity Foundation in a variety of contexts. For example, we now offer an ongoing series of E-Programs featuring dialogues by Master Charles on a wide range of conscious living topics.

Additionally, we are always involved in ongoing research and development of new programs, products and services that enhance and refine The Synchronicity Experience, always with a view towards the most precision application of modern technologies of balance and vibrational entrainment. As such technologies become available, they are incorporated into Synchronicity Conscious Living Integrative Lifestyle. In this way, we remain on the cutting edge of modern technological innovation and application in the field of human transformational experience. Thus, we remain dedicated to the ongoing unfoldment of Master Charles' original intention in creating The Synchronicity Experience nearly twenty years ago.

An Invitation to You - Come Join the Celebration in Wholeness and Fulfillment

Conscious Living or living with balance in an imbalanced world is the primary challenge we face as human beings in today's world. In this book, we have delineated, in a concise presentation, what The Synchronicity Experience has to offer to anyone who endeavors to live consciously. Balanced, holistic awareness and human fulfillment are the hallmarks of a conscious living integrative lifestyle and for nearly twenty years we have demonstrated that this contemporary approach to human transformation delivers this experience to anyone who applies it with consistency.

Whether you are a seasoned meditator, looking for a more expanded experience of holistic awareness, or just starting out on your transformational journey..... there are products, programs and services within The Synchronicity Experience that are created especially for you. Everything we offer is based on Synchronicity Holodynamic vibrational entrainment technology and is designed to deliver balance, wholeness and fulfillment to human experience. We cordially invite you to come and join with us in a celebration in wholeness and fulfillment and welcome you in the awareness of our Oneness.

For more information on
The Synchronicity Experience.....

Synchronicity Foundation International
P.O. Box 694
Nellysford, Virginia 22958
(434) 361-2323
1-800-962-2033

E-mail: synch@synchronicity.org
Web-site: www.synchronicity.org